WAL
SOU
AN

by
Olive Brown
and
Jean Whittaker

GRIBUN

Brown & Whittaker
2005 Revised and updated

Carsaig Cliffs from Scoor

CONTENTS

Public Road	=
Route of Walk...............	.....
Bridge	⊨
Gate..............................	⊢
Summit	△
Deciduous Trees.............	♧
Coniferous Trees...........	♣
Viewpoint......................	ⵕ
Fence.............................	+—+—+
Dun	ⵣ

© Olive M. Brown and E. Jean Whittaker, 1987

ISBN 1904353061

A CODE FOR MULL

1. Gates
Farmers say that when walkers cross their land gates cause more problems than anything else, so we would ask, on their behalf, that you respect these rules:

    1 If you find a gate open, leave it open.
    2 If you find a gate closed, shut it after you again, securely fastened and stockproof.
    3 If you find a gate locked or tied up with string or wire, please don't try to open it. Climb it at the hinge end.

2. Dogs:
Dogs also cause problems for farmers so we would ask you to keep your dog under control where there are animals and to take special note of the lambing season (March to May) when sheep should not be disturbed. If you find any animal in distress such as an apparently lost lamb or a sheep stuck on a ledge, report it, do not attempt to deal with it yourself.

4. Deer:
Most of south Mull is stalked. Difficulties between stalkers and walkers usually arise through simple ignorance and lack of awareness that deer form an important part of the Highland economy, just as sheep do. There are only a few walks in this book where the walker is likely to come into conflict with the stalking interest and these have been indicated. The walker in Scotland enjoys a most enviable freedom. In order that that freedom may continue for the sake of other walkers, we have suggested that certain walks be avoided altogether for a restricted period during the height of the stalking season. Thereafter, some culling takes place and it might be advisable to check with the appropriate landowner whether stalking is in progress. A rifle bullet travels three miles - you could get shot!

4. Go carefully on single track roads. The passing places are for vehicles to pass or to allow overtaking. Never park there or anywhere where it is likely to cause difficulty of access to farmers' fields.

5 Respect wildlife, plants and trees and guard against fire.

6. Leave no litter.

Leaflets about the new Scottish Outdoor Access Code are available from Tourist Offices.

Ben More and the Chioch from the Glen road.

INTRODUCTION

Hills, glens, rocky coasts, sandy beaches - the south part of the island of Mull offers the walker a great variety of routes and scenery. With such richness to choose from it is, perhaps, not easy to know where to start. This book gives a selection of different walks ranging from the lonely hills of central Mull to the gentle island of Iona. Each walk has been thoroughly explored by the authors and a sketch map and an indication of the time taken is given. This timing is fairly generous, allowing for stops to admire the view or even where necessary, to catch your breath! Taking along an Ordnance Survey map of the area will be useful, either the Landranger Series (Sheets 48 and 49) or better still for walking the Pathfinder Series (Sheets 329, 330, 341, 342, 343 and 353) or the new format Explorer 373 and 375.

Although geology shapes the scenery everywhere, here in south Mull there are dramatic contrasts round every corner. The evidence of a landscape formed by volcanic eruptions and moulded by glaciers is everywhere to be seen, scarcely softened by man. Geological curiosities abound in south Mull, the best known being the Carsaig Arches and MacCulloch's Tree. Whilst the geological structure forms the bones of the island, the pattern of land use has changed and is changing. The vast crofting population of the nineteenth century has gone, their inheritors are the farmers and estate owners of today, with fish farming a more recent addition to the economy. Subsistence farming has been replaced by a type of farming which aims at a quality market - prime Scotch beef, lamb, venison and salmon. It is worth remembering that the wide open spaces beloved of the walker are in use. In particular, sporting estates must be managed like any other business. There is little hardship in avoiding the hills during the height of the stalking season when Mull has coastal walking second to none, and we would ask you to read most carefully note 3 on Deer in the Code for Mull on page 4.

Of the many coastal walks in south Mull and Iona, no two are alike and each is rewarding in its own way, whether it has dramatic cliffs or gentle wooded shores. The sea is never very far away, even when on an inland walk, and views to other distant islands can be seen from many vantage points.

Even on the best of summer days, it is advisable to wear sturdy footwear, as much of the land is peaty and boggy and the coastal walking can be very rough. A waterproof jacket and an extra sweater should be carried against a sudden change of weather as some of the walks take you into remote country. If you have a car, please park it thoughtfully, not in a passing place, on the road or in a farmer's gateway.

The descriptions of the walks may mention things of the past by way of interest, such as deserted villages or legends of ancient feuds, but the island of Mull is alive and growing, and a place of work to its inhabitants - please do not jeopardise anyone's livelihood by careless behaviour. We are indebted to the farmers and landowners over whose land you will pass, and we must thank them for their co-operation and helpful advice. Please read the Code for Mull . . . and enjoy your walking!

Olive Brown   *Tobermory*
Jean Whittaker   *Spring 2005*

1. Glen More

The road from Craignure to Kinloch has been improved and straightened over the years, leaving sections of the meandering old road which are pleasant to walk along. The most continuous stretch of this old road is the seven miles from Ardura to Craig, passing through Glen More and enlivened with old stories: some true, some traditional. In the summer the Iona service bus passes close to the walk every two hours, so that the walker can either return to the start or continue to the Ross of Mull.

A little beyond the turn off to Lochbuie and Croggan, there is a cattle grid and, just short of this, it is possible to take the car down on to the old road to park. The road follows the valley of the Lussa through trees for nearly two miles. About three-quarters of a mile upstream is the Pedlar's Pool, where there is a memorial, dated April 1st 1891, to the pedlar, John Jones, who died of smallpox contracted when selflessly nursing a stricken family on his round.

A true but sad story. The next story is purely legend and tells how the huge boulder which lies above Ishriff came to be called Clach Sguabain. This boulder was thrown from Loch Spelve during the course of an argument between the legendary Fingalian giants, Sguabain and Neacail. The boulder thrown in return sits near Croggan perched on a rock by the shore.

The heart of the glen may be said to be around the chain of three lochs which are visible from the road. In the nearest of the lochs, Loch Sguabain, is an island. The island is a prehistoric construction known as a crannog, being wholly or partly artificial and occupied into historic times. It is associated with the character of Eoghann a Chinn Bhig (Ewan of the Little Head) who figures at the centre of Mull's creepiest supernatural story. Ewan, son and heir of Lochbuie, lived in a castle on this island with his wife, who was forever nagging him to obtain more land (and, no doubt, a more salubrious dwelling place) from his father. Lochbuie proved unforthcoming. High words passed, Ewan struck him, and a clan battle was in the making. On the eve of the battle, Ewan

met up with a fairy woman and asked her his destiny. The reply predictably was enigmatic: if Ewan's wife offered him butter and cheese before the battle, unasked and with her own hand, all would be well. If not, Ewan would die. On the morning of the battle both Ewan and his wife ran true to form: his wife stayed in bed and Ewan, foolish to the last, waited in vain for the loving words until he could delay no longer but went out to face his father and his father's ally, MacLean of Duart, on the battlefield. There, as foretold, he was killed, his head sliced from his shoulders by a claymore. His headless trunk, still upright in the stirrups, was carried by his terrified horse to the ford in the Lussa, where the body finally fell out of the saddle. You can see Ewan's island home in Loch Sguabain but before that, at Torness, you are at the very spot where Ewan fell from his horse. There, buried in the heather on the right of the path that leads down to the ford, you may see the cairn that Ewan's servants built on the spot where he fell to earth. His corpse was conveyed to Iona where it was buried but hardly laid to rest - Ewan still rides abroad in the southern parts of Mull and the sight and sound of the headless horseman is said to presage a death among the family of the MacLaines of Lochbuie.

By way of a more pleasant ending to this tale of horror, the walker might like to go a little downstream from the ford (now bridged) and admire the Falls of Lussa - a noted spot to see salmon running.

Where Glen More is at its narrowest and steep cliffs rise up to each side, there is a feeling of loneliness better appreciated on foot than from a car or bus. Deer are often seen here grazing quite near the road, and eagles and buzzards may well be seen soaring above. Even in the days when Mull had more people living in scattered villages than today, few people lived around here and it was at this lonely place that David Balfour, the hero of *Kidnapped*, had a strange encounter with a blind beggar who carried a pistol and who could "shoot by ear at several yards" and who tried to rob him of the little money he had left.

After the old road reaches Craig, with a fine view of Ben More, the stretches accessible for walking are so few and intermittent that it is better to return to the new road, or retrace the old road the way you have come.

Loch Spelve

2. Croggan

9 miles, 4 hours

A gentle coastal walk along the shores of a sheltered sea loch, mostly on a quiet road. Loch Spelve, almost landlocked and girt with bracken-clad hills might have been lifted from the Trossachs or the Lake District.

Start at Kinlochspelve at the junction on the Craignure to Lochbuie road signposted to Croggan. You may, of course, shorten this walk by any distance you desire by driving part, or all of the way to Croggan but the road is pleasant, fringed with birch trees and is easy level walking following the coastline all the way past Croggan Pier. Beyond Croggan, the road becomes a track, bottomed with the rounded pebbles of the raised beach over which it runs. Not far from Croggan there is an amazing rock known as Clach Neacail (Nicol's Stone), shaped like a mushroom, a little below HW mark. Geologists will tell you that this is a perched block left by an ancient glacier. Legend says it was thrown from Loch Spelve by a giant. Out in the channel the water is in a constant state of motion, funnelled in and out of the narrow entrance at a rate of four knots springs. A white spot on a rock on the opposite shore is a navigation mark for boats negotiating the entrance: in days gone by MacBrayne's steamers (much smaller vessels in those days than the massive MV *Isle of Mull*) came into the loch for a scheduled stop at Croggan pier. When Croggan Pier was completed in 1896, Croggan's bard, Lachann Livingstone, wrote a Gaelic praise poem to it.

Follow the track past a sandy beach to where it ends at a house called Portfield. As you work along the Firth of Lorn, there are views across the Firth towards Kerrera and the hills south of Oban.

These may be better appreciated by climbing up the hill, Maol Buidhe, behind Portfield where the track ends. At Portfield there are notices requesting walkers to avoid going too close to the house - please respect these and the owners' privacy. Climb up behind the house, following the route indicated, pausing from time to time to enjoy the views across the Firth of Lorn. Make for the summit of Maol Buidhe, a grassy dome, where the view now extends from Lismore to the Garvellochs where St Columba's mother is said to be buried.

Continue across the high ground towards the mouth of Loch Spelve and descend to the deserted villages of Barnashoag and Balgamrie, which show evidence of having been quite large communities. From here follow the interesting old wall back down to the track - turn left to return to the start.

3. Gualacholish

Start at the gate on the south side of the A849, half a mile past Oakbank. There is a fairly good track all the way, although it runs with water after rainy spell, making its way through low hills, gradually rising then dipping down to cross a small river near the ruins of Killean. Continue to the top of hill to the more substantial ruins of Gualacholish. This is not the usual scatter of small houses but a substantial 19th century house with barns and outbuildings. It was built as the manse with glebe for minister of the parish of Torosay but when a new manse was built at the more central location of Craignure it then became a farm. There is an interesting hollow tree in front of the house.

Killean graveyard

9

To get to the burial ground of Killean, set off west following a very old wall, which twice meets another wall - bear right each time and suddenly you are in sight of the graveyard with a ruined chapel. If you are thinking that this cemetery is a long way from any road, consider that coffins were brought by sea from Croggan and Lochbuie, landing on the shore where there is a grassy slope. Among those who came that way and is buried here is the bard Lachann Livingstone of Croggan.

Now retrace your steps to Gualacholish and rejoin the track, following the wall down to the sea through gentle birch woods. Bear left at the shore and enjoy a stretch of pleasant level walking with caves and the sea spouting up between gaps in the rocks. You are very likely to encounter some wild goats, perhaps with young kids at heel. They will probably give you a considered stare before ambling off up a steep path, knowing they can always reach a ledge inaccessible to humans. Continue until reaching a gate, leaving it as you find it, and cross the river to the sandy bay called Port Donain. Above the shore, in the long grass and bracken are two kerb cairns, possibly Bronze Age and a tiny tombstone to a dog.

Port Donain

Carry on to the farmyard at Auchnacraig, please be thoughtful as you pass through farmyard, turn left on to the tarmac and it is now about two miles back to the start. As you cross the old arched bridge, built about 1790, stop and look down, as you might catch a glimpse of an otter, and there are usually swans, and greenshank in the spring. Just near the junction with the main road at Lochdonhead is the Free Church. The Free Church broke away from the Church of Scotland at the "Disruption" in 1843, but the landowner, or heritor as landowners were termed, would not allow the congregation to meet on his lands, so they met huddled in a tent in a gravel pit between low and high water, and therefore not on his land, to hear their minister preach. At the main road turn left to complete the circuit - how many deer did you see on this walk?

4. Glen Forsa

8 miles, 3 hours

Stalking: Contact Brian Fraser, Keeper, 01680 300407

This walk takes you from the outskirts of Salen through to the Glen More road and is almost entirely level. Though barely 8 miles on foot, the journey round by car is at least nineteen miles. It is possible to do this walk as a two-car expedition or by using the buses to return to your car.

Leave the A849 Salen to Craignure road just where it splits briefly into a dual carriageway, a mile beyond Salen near the Glenforsa Hotel. Please park where indicated. Visitors are welcome to walk in the glen unless stalking is in progress (see above). The straight track runs side by side with the Forsa, a noted salmon river, and through several gates with stiles for walkers. Ahead is the steep cone of Ben Talaidh where the wreckage of a wartime plane still lies in the central gully (see page 12).

Four miles from the start, the track runs uphill, goes through a ford and then forks. At the fork a propeller from the plane has been set up as a memorial to those who died in the crash. From this slight rise look back down the glen, a classic example of a U-shaped glaciated valley with its abundant moraines.

The right hand fork leads up to the bothy at Tomsleibhe belonging to the Mountain Bothy Association, and on to the gruelling pass through to Loch Ba, but bear left to continue through Glen Forsa. Another gate leads into a plantation and the forestry track continues for some distance before giving way to a well trodden path and another gate. After a stile you will reach an electric fence where a gate will take you out on to the open hill at a block of open ground left as a corridor for deer commuting between the two hills. Just beyond this the hillside bends away back into the Coire Ghaibhre. Walk along the contour above the fence until you reach a place where two burns from this corrie meet and plunge into a deep gorge crossed by the fence. Make your way a little upstream to cross both burns, then re-enter the plantation by another gate. Lower down the burn can be seen the remains of some ruined cottages where several families once lived. From here follow the burn down as far as the second ruined cottage, turn right, and follow the ride through the forest until you come to another spur of forestry track which will take you the last half mile to the road. This is a convenient place to park if walking from the opposite direction, but starting from the Salen end gives more interesting views of Ben Talaidh and of remote corries on the far side of the glen.

11

5. Ben Talaidh 761m

Stalking: Contact Brian Fraser, Keeper, 01680 300407

This lovely, cone-shaped mountain is easily recognised from many viewpoints in Mull and can be climbed from either a north or south approach. From its steep sides flow the burns that feed three river systems: the Forsa, the Ba and the Lussa. Its short turf is a delight to walk on in dry conditions: in wet, it leads to many an impromptu glissade!

Ascent from the north

The Tomsleibhe bothy, four miles up Glen Forsa, marks the beginning of the ascent. The bothy is a good place to pause, after the long walk in, to read other walkers' comments the bothy book, before setting off for the summit. The easiest line of ascent is the most obvious - the walker crosses the Allt nan Clar and follows the north ridge to the top, pausing from time to time to look back down the glaciated valley of the Forsa and beyond to the Sound of Mull.

At the summit take note that it is the cairn and not the trig pillar that marks the highest point. After a recent resurvey there is some dispute among "Corbett" hunters as to whether Ben Talaidh now qualifies as a hill over 2500 feet. Routes down can be either by retracing the ascent route, or by picking your way down over the scree on the east side to the shoulder and then following the Allt nan Clar down Glen Lean back to the bothy. The bed of this burn is scattered with the remains of a Dakota that crashed during the war. The plane was a Dakota DC3 on a flight from Canada to Prestwick. On 1st February 1945, unable to maintain altitude due to severe air frame icing, it clipped the summit of the mountain and slid down the north side. Of the eight people aboard, three were killed but five survived. A massive rescue

Ben Talaidh from Torness

operation was mounted by the local doctor, shepherds and police, with the help of navy personnel from the large wartime base at Tobermory. For some time the plane remained on the slope of the hill, relatively intact but, after some years, a decision was made to break up the wreck and the remains were pushed down to the bed of the Allt nan Clar. A memorial scroll with information about this tragedy is hanging in the entrance hall of Salen School and there is a display in the Mull Museum in Tobermory.

Ascent from Glen More

The ascent from the south avoids a long walk in. Ben Talaidh is the third highest hill on Mull after Ben More (966m) and Dun da Ghaoithe (766m) but any route to its summit is short and steep. Start at the forestry track half a mile west of the ruin of Torness on the long bend in the A849 in Glen More. Walk up the north bank of the Abhainn Doir a Mhaim keeping to the edge of the trees until you reach a stile which gives access to the open hillside. From here it is a very steep pull up onto the ridge. As you walk round the curve of the ridge, the three river valleys lead the eye away to the distant sea. Now a steady ascent of about 700 feet brings you out onto the rounded top with its trig pillar and cairn.

The descent can be varied by coming down the steep and unpleasant scree slope as far as the col between Ben Talaidh and Beinn Beag to have a look at the site of the Dakota crash, then down through Coire Ghaibhre. Go though the gate and back along Glen Forsa to Glen More as described on page 11.

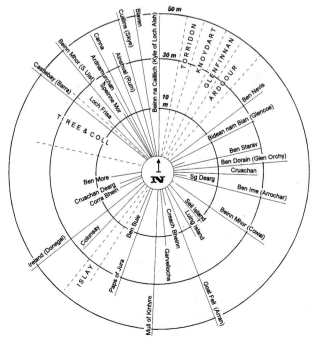

6. Dun da Ghaoithe Ridge   *An all day excursion*

This classic ridge walk is one of the best in Mull and takes in Dun da Ghaoithe. At 766m (2513 feet) it is the second highest of the Mull hills and is a "Corbett". The hill welcomes the visitor to Mull as it dominates the approach to Craignure. Its Gaelic name means hill of the two winds and perhaps it was named by sailors as it deflects the winds up the Firth of Lorn and the Sound of Mull. Certainly its summit and the long ridge leading northwards from it offer an incomparable view of these two stretches of water as well as fine prospects of the central Mull mountains.

From Craignure, take the A849 Fionnphort road and, just past the main entrance to Torosay Castle, turn off on the right hand side of the road up a narrow cutting. Fork right almost immediately and follow the road until it reaches a locked gate near a farm. There is room to park here.

Cross the sturdy stile, helpfully put there by the landowner, and walk up the road to the first of two telecommunications masts, then on up to the second transmitter tower. The road is very steep but you will want to stop frequently to admire the views across to Duart Castle and beyond to Oban and Lorn. Looking north Ben Nevis, the Mamores and the peaks of Glencoe can also be seen clearly, when the weather is right. By this time you are two thirds of the way up as you strike off due west for the summit of Dun da Ghaoithe, skirting the curved cliff of crags at the head of Coire nan Each. As always, the appearance of a trig pillar is a welcome sight but this pillar and the cairn behind are not yet the summit which lies half a mile away to the NW and 30 feet higher.

From the summit follow the ridge in a north westerly line, taking care to follow as the ridge curves to the left on the way to Beinn Thunicaraidh the next summit. The ridge traverses over a series of little tops, rocky mounds and around lochans - Beinn Thunicaraidh, Beinn Mheadhon, to the last top, Beinn a Chreagach Mhor, the first top to dip below 2000 feet. The views change here - the Sound of Mull, which has been a constant companion on the right hand, now swings away directly ahead of you to Tobermory and there are new and spectacular views through the gap made by Loch na Keal to Staffa, Little Colonsay and the Treshnish Islands, northwards to Loch Frisa, up the Sound of Mull to Calve Island off Tobermory and beyond to Ardnamurchan, with the possibility of a glimpse of Rum and Skye on a clear day. Across the Sound lies Morvern and the village of Lochaline, where a mine produces very fine sand for industrial use, and there are the old and new Ardtornish castles. You may see a small freighter negotiating the narrow entrance to join the ceaseless traffic plying the Sound of Mull: CalMac ferries heading for the Outer Isles, ore carriers taking rock from the Glensanda quarries to engineering projects around the world, smaller cargo boats, fishing boats and yachts of all sizes sailing up the Sound.

The ridge at this end is by no means as clear as it appears on the map and from the top of Beinn Chreagach Mhor, care must be taken. To avoid the bands of nasty little cliffs, leave the summit taking a line on the distant village of Lochaline across the sound of Mull and walk on till a line of old fence posts is reached. Keep with this fence until an ancient metal gate is reached then make for the final top of the ridge, Maol Bhuidhe. This detour avoids the worst of an area of boggy ground interspersed with peat hags which is so tiring to walk through. Taking a line on the shingle bar at the mouth of the Forsa river, head for a rocky knoll with a green skirt above Pennygown cemetery. Descend to the road near the cemetery after what has been a splendid high level walk.

Other descents may be made. The first opportunity is to go down the north side of the Allt an Dubh Coire going down the ridge until a deer fence is reached. The gate is across the river just below some fine waterfalls. Re-cross the river and continue down keeping above and to the west of the green fields of Scallastle farm to reach the main road at another gate

There are several ways to tackle this hill using the buses or a combination of car and bus. Service buses connect the start and finish of the walk with the ferry at Craignure every two hours in summer (see timetable). It is therefore possible to drop off the ridge at many points and catch one of these buses to return to your starting point. It is also possible from Craignure to reach Torosay Castle by narrow gauge railway or a woodland walk.

MISTY MOUNTAIN WAYPOINT GUIDE				
GRID REF	HEIGHT metres	NAME OF WAYPOINT	BEARING ° TO NEXT WAYPOINT	miles (approx)
723348	80	STILE (Starting point)	unsurfaced road	2½
694352	431	MAOL NAN UAN (upper mast)	270°	1
676353	754	TRIG PILLAR	335°	½
673363	766	DUN DA GHAOITHE SUMMIT	320°	½
669367	630	CORNER OF RIDGE	275°	½
661369	648	BEINN THUNICARAIDH	325°	¾
654378	637	BEINN MHEADHON	300°	1
642386	500	LOCH A'MHAIM (AT FENCE)	290°	¾
631391	579	BEINN CHREAGACH MHOR	40°	¼
634395	500	FENCE	follow fence to old gate	1
629410	350	GATE IN FENCE	300°	¼
624413	368	MAOL BHUIDHE	310°	1
608427	100	KNOLL	310°	½
604433	30	PENNYGOWN CEMETERY		finish

7. Glen Clachaig

6 miles, 4 hours

For stalking information telephone 0131 226 2500 (Season August - October 20)

This route is one of the ancient drove roads used to move cattle from one part of Mull to another. Beef cattle (usually called `black` whatever their colour) were the mainstay of the Highland economy up till the 19th century. From as early as the 16th century it is known that cattle were shipped from Coll and Tiree and landed at Croig and Kintra. From there they were driven through the glens of Mull, grazing as they went. In Glen Bellart there was one of the largest fairs in the West Highlands where, three times a year, cattle dealers congregated from all over the country. In the mid-eighteenth century, Mull exported about 2000 cattle a year. Most of these went out through Grass Point and were shipped by way of the island of Kerrera to the mainland. The shortest sea crossings were chosen as well as the best grazing on the way, in order to get the cattle to the trysts (markets) at Crieff and Falkirk in the best condition possible.

Start at Knock on the prominent bend in the road just after the hump backed bridge over the River Ba, where the track leads into the Ben More estates. Immediately on leaving the road, bear right through a gate, where notices give details of the stalking season on this estate. A stony track leads along the shores of Loch Ba through old birch woods for about two miles. The valley opens out on to a wide plain surrounded by hills. Here, if anywhere, the explorer feels at the heart of Mull's ancient volcanic drama. Here, about 60 million years ago, a magma reservoir pushed upwards in a huge dome but when the pressure was released through a ring-shaped crack, the centre subsided much like a failed soufflé.

About half-way up the loch, the drove road forks to the right at a cairn. The track continues till it crosses a burn below a ruined cottage - the bridge has been washed away, but if the water at the ford is too deep, then there is the remains of an old bridge beside a rowan tree about thirty yards downstream. The next burn, the Allt Beithe, should be crossed close to where it flows into the River Clachaig. Just downstream are two small round stone enclosures. These are sheep buchts or twinning pens where orphaned lambs are bonded to a foster mother. Upstream the ford across the Clachaig river is marked by a small cairn on a level patch of grass, and in wet weather can be kneedeep. Some of the drovers of old were mounted on small ponies, but crossing rivers was always a problem.

By now the Chioch has come into view, dominating the head of the valley, and on the other side of the col is Cruachan Dearg mirroring the Chioch in its conical shape. Walking in the valley bottom is heavy going through the luxuriant moor grass which provides rough grazing for cattle right up to the head of the valley, though the large hairy Highland cattle of today are at least twice the size of the wiry black cattle which were driven over this pass in the old droving days.

From the ford, the path goes steadily uphill to the top of the pass, with, here and there, the old stone edging of the drove road visible through the grass. In the 18th century, landlords had to provide statute labour for the building and maintenance of roads. The tenants from Lagganulva to Killiechronan worked on this road.

At the summit of the pass (1085) feet) stands the Carn Cul Righ Albainn (Cairn with its Back to Scotland). Tradition has it that this cairn marked the boundary between the Picts and the Scots. The path from here to the Glen road is well made and descends by a steady gradient, at first through the hanging valley of the Allt Teanga Brideig and then by a sharp descent to the road, with views of the Coladoir River meandering to its estuary at Loch Scridain.

Head of Loch Ba

8. Burg and the Fossil Tree

10 miles, 7 hours
An all-day excursion

At the end of the Ardmeanach peninsula, MacCulloch's Tree, the fossilised cast of a tree growing over 50 million years ago, was discovered by the geologist John MacCulloch in 1819.

From the B8035 take the turning to Tiroran, passing behind Tiroran House. This section of the route is well waymarked by the National Trust until you are delivered safely into the Trust's car park, 2¾ miles along the road (cars may not be taken any further). Despite all this, it is still a walk into untamed scenery - long and at times hard going, but full of interesting geological features and wild land and seascapes. Goats and red deer can be seen and buzzards and eagles hunt along the cliffs. Pass through the gate by the car park and follow the track on past Tavool house, then on another mile to Burg Farm (Chrissie's Cottage).

Just past the farm is Dun Bhuirg, an early fortified structure and one of many duns around the coast of Mull. Within its walls is a memorial to Daisy Cheape drowned on August 15, 1896. The Cheape family owned Tiroran and Carsaig estates and the accident occurred when Daisy, then twelve, her brothers and boatmen set out on a very wild day to sail round to Carsaig, the dinghy taking the party out to embark capsized and sadly Daisy did not survive. Pause to read her memorial and to look back up Loch Scridain to the saddle-backed summit of Ben Buie.

From here, the path crosses a grassy area, once cultivated, before it begins to climb up and follow the side of the hill. It is a fairly narrow track and requires care in places. Along this stretch some of the unusual formations of basalt columns can be seen. On the island of Staffa these hexagonal columns are mostly vertical but here they lie horizontal, or in a fan shape, in one place like the spokes of a wheel and in another laid down like bottles in a wine cellar. Looking down on these from the path above is more rewarding than the closer view you can get by scrambling down to the shore.

The path now continues at the same level until it ends in a short downward slope (care should be taken) to the head of a steel ladder running down 20 feet of cliff and giving access to the final section of bouldery beach. After that it is a scramble along the shore - agates can sometimes be found here. There are two waterfalls falling down from the high cliffs in parallel symmetry. These, which can be seen from as far away as Iona, are markers for the tree which lies just beyond. The outline of the trunk is moulded in the lava face to the left of a cave mouth and the shape and size of this trunk, 40 feet high and 5 feet across, is that of a massive tree. This tree was large enough to exert a cooling

effect on the lava by which it was engulfed with the result that the surrounding columns of basalt have been bent towards it. At the base, about four feet from the ground, there can be seen the dark charcoal remains of

One of the twin waterfalls

the timber from when it was overwhelmed by hot lava, and at one time much more of this black deposit was visible. Eroded by fossil hunters over the years, only the hollow shape now exists. Please do not be tempted to damage this unique fossil any further.

From the tree the usual route back is to retrace your steps along the shore, up the ladder and along the path to Burg and Tiroran.

It should be noted that going beyond the tree is a major undertaking - the headland being only negotiable at low water or by a difficult and potentially dangerous route further up. The north side of the peninsula is some of the most broken and difficult country in Mull.

9. Ben Buie

right717 m, 2352 ft

Restricted period mid-August to mid-October

Ben Buie is another of the hills on Mull that gives the climber the total satisfaction of starting from sea level and climbing every one of the 2352 feet to the summit. It dominates the loch and village which carry the same name buidhe (boo-ee) meaning yellow. Its glacis of grass and scree rising to a summit dome of crag is unmistakable as you come down the winding road to Loch Buie. What is not evident from the road is that there are, in fact, two summits and that the area between them and to the NE of the second summit is a terrain of lumpy ground crossed by little rock bands. In mist this broken country is confusing and the fact that crags and cliffs await the unwary on SW, SE and E sides makes the top of Ben Buie a bad place to get lost: there is a local magnetic anomaly and the compass should not be relied upon.

Leave the Lochbuie road at the telephone box and follow the fairly well worn route up the left side of the burn, crossing some smaller burns on the way. Height is quickly gained on the continuously steep slope and each pause for breath will give you time to admire the widening views of the waters of Loch Buie. At the head of the loch you will see Laggan Sands, Moy Castle and the wide spread of level ground behind Lochbuie House. As you get higher, Loch Uisg comes into view to the southeast and there is a wide panorama over towards Oban and Lorn.

From about 1700 feet, rough scree demands careful footwork to avoid starting an avalanche of stones. The last 100 feet look formidable from below and gazing upwards the walker may be excused for wondering whether there is a way up through the crags which girdle the summit, but there is a shallow rake running from left to right which takes you to within a few feet of the southern and higher top. The summit cairn is a fairly substantial one and affords shelter while you admire the wide views of the other hills of Mull. Across Beinn nan Gobhar to the west you can see Gorrie's Leap, at the top of the high cliffs above the Carsaig Arches. To the north lies Ben More while to the northeast are Cruachan Dearg, Corra Bheinn and Ben Talaidh, all inviting climbs some other day.

Descent by the steep route of the ascent is rather remorseless and a more varied way down may be found by walking across to the second summit a quarter of a mile away. From the second summit continue north, to avoid the precipitous east face and pick your way down into Coire nan Each. Before going down, make sure you can see the line of descent almost clear to the valley floor at the southern end of the loch. Here you are joining the old path through from Glen More to Lochbuie and the return to the road is described on page 22.

A Beginner's Hill Flora

For anyone just starting to take an interest in plant life, the hill country of Mull is a good place to begin. The acid soils and the high rainfall produce a distinctive flora with few surprises and, for the beginner, reassuringly few species. The budding botanist taking to the Mull hills should be able to tick off the following 50 species without delaying the rest of the party and pronounce them typical of the western hills of Scotland.

Ten for starters
Ivy
Foxglove
Honeysuckle
Rowan
Harebell
Thyme
Bracken
Cross-leaved Heath
Bell Heather
Ling

Plants of the hill slopes
Heath Bedstraw
Bilberry
Bugle
Cowberry
Eyebright
Hard Fern
Parsley Fern
Herb Robert
St John's Wort

Heath Spotted Orchid
Milkwort
Sea Plantain
Devil's Bit Scabious
Selfheal
Heath Speedwell
Tormentil
Bird's Foot Trefoil
Bitter Vetch

Plants of the tops
Alpine Ladies Mantle
Cat's Foot
Moss Campion
Sea Pearlwort
Rhacomitrium (Moss)
Roseroot
Selaginella Selaginoides
Starry Saxifrage
English Stonecrop
Thrift

Water Plants
Bog Bean
Potomogeton Sp
Water Lobelia

Plants of the boggy ground
Bog Asphodel
Butterwort
Cottongrass
Sun Dew
Grass of Parnassus
Lousewort
Bog Myrtle

10. Circuit of Ben Buie

Restricted period end August-end October

This long circuit round the base of Ben Buie, the highest hill south of the Glen More road, gives a fine appreciation of the desolate country around Glen More, that great glacier gouged slice through Mull which separates north and central Mull from the Ross and the extreme south.

Leave the A849 at the highest point, 11 miles west of Craignure, (grid ref NM616303) above the chain of three lochs. Walk, keeping well up the hill, towards the gap between Loch an Ellen and Loch Airdeglais. Ford the burn which connects the two lochs and pick up the good path on the other side. This goes all the way to Loch Buie, with the long eastern flank of Ben Buie rising steadily on the walker's right hand.

In the shallow col the path crosses some boggy ground and in two places a series of stepping stones has been laid at some time, as useful now as when they were put in position. Just before the path starts its final descent to Loch Buie it crosses the Abhainn a`Chaiginn Mhoir and the walker should be alert not to miss the crossing place. The path passes close to a distinctive pyramidal mound. Ford the river about 50 yards beyond. The path now descends sharply between large black ice-smoothed rocks. From here you can see down to the flat lands round Lochbuie, and out to sea lies the island of Colonsay, with Islay and Jura beyond. There is a ruggedness about this last mile of descent - the Gleann a`Chaiginn Mhoir, or valley of the rough terrain - and at the point where the path joins the road, Ben Buie presents its most spectacular aspect, girdled with crags and dominating the few houses at its feet. The path meets the road through a metal gate 20 yards east of a fine old stone bridge.

With the use of two cars it is possible to terminate the walk here. There is much of interest to see at Lochbuie. See page 24.

To continue the walk, turn right where the path joins the road and walk over the bridge and past the houses of Lochbuie. The road reaches the sea at a curious triangular monument erected by Lochbuie and his Highlanders to commemorate the coronation of King Edward VII and Queen Alexandra. Turn right again here and continue until, just after a burn is bridged, there is a gate and a sign indicating the public footpath to Carsaig. However, turn right yet again and go up the hill to some farm buildings and out onto the hillside beyond. Climb steadily through the woodland for about half a mile until below the craggy end of Beinn nan Gobhar. The path now forks, one path leading gently down and along the wall (see page 25, the Horse Track), the right-hand fork leading up the hill. Keeping ever to the right, now tackle the rise up to the Bealach an t-Sidhein (pass of the fairies) pausing, as you will feel the need to do quite regularly, to look back at the view of Loch Buie and beyond. Once Loch Buie has disappeared you will have the satisfaction of knowing that the hard work of ascent has been done. For the next mile the walker works gently round the contour with the crags of Ben Buie to his right and the dramatic valley of Glenbyre to his left.

When the head of the valley is about half a mile off, the crags come to an end and there is a minute and reedy lochan to the right of the path. You should leave the path at this point and make for the summit of Cruach nan Con (1626 feet). Ben Buie, lost to view since turning up Glenbyre, comes back into sight, now showing its western aspect over the waters of Loch Fuaran. To the left of it is the symmetrical top of Ben Talaidh and the weary walker may be interested to know that your car lies directly below it. But if at this point you think the rest is a formality, you are sadly mistaken. The descent from Cruach nan Con over Torr a Ghoai into the valley of the Abhainn Loch Fuaran (itself a problem in spate) and the walk down to the road are the roughest two miles in the whole round. Even the sheep do not reckon much to this as walking country and you are left to plough your own pathless and trackless way through the endless hummocky moraines until you finally reach the valley floor and are faced with the choice of fording the Coladoir River or following it up to the watershed between it and the River Lussa. There is no bridge now at Craig. Only the fine panorama of the hills north of the Glen road relieves this last section and the tarmac was never so welcome as on the last stretch back to the car. An excellent round despite the sting in the tail.

11. Short excursions around Lochbuie

1. Laggan Sands and Mausoleum

Shortly after passing Loch Uisg on the road to Lochbuie there is a lodge and white gates. Turn left through the gates and then left again, where the road forks. Follow the twists and turns of the road down to the sea, turning left yet again at the junction where the sea is reached. The wide sweep of Laggan Sands are a quarter of a mile beyond, backed by the open grassy space where the car may be parked.

The Mausoleum for the MacLaines of Lochbuie is an interesting objective for a short stroll from the beach. The chapel is mediaeval in origin but had fallen into disuse by 1701, the date of the first burial. It was considerably restored in 1864 and again in 1972. It may be reached by the track that runs along the top of the beach.

2. Moy Castle

Although Moy Castle is within easy walking distance of Laggan Sands, the more usual approach is from the end of Loch Buie village. From the Post Office, follow the track east along the shore to a small car park. Continue down the track, over the bridge, through the field gate and along the marked path. The castle, although apparently in a good state of preservation, is unsafe and is kept locked for that reason. This MacLaine stronghold dates from at least the early 15th century and continued to be lived in until 1752 when the new mansion nearby was built. This is a private house and not open to the public.

STONE CIRCLE
LOCHBUIE

3. Stone Circle

This is the only stone circle on Mull. The circle consists of eight stones with the place of a ninth marked by a boulder and an isolated stone a few feet away. There are also two other stones in the vicinity and a kerb cairn in a group of trees.

To reach these monuments, keep on for the houses of Lochbuie past the turning for Laggan Sands and leave your car at the stone bridge over the Abhainn a'Chaiginn Mhoir. Go through the wicket gate and follow the white stones towards the line of trees, making for the obvious clump or grove in this line and crossing a small wooden bridge in the field (there is a standing stone some distance to the left of this). From the grove a track goes towards a fence which comes in from the left with a gate in it marked "Stone Circle". As you approach the circle, note that there are outliers - isolated stones at some distance away. To an observer in the middle of the circle, the setting sun of the winter solstice goes down over the tallest of these outliers.

4. The Horse Track

The shore road to Glenbyre was built at the beginning of the century, carved out from the rugged and broken coast. The older route in was by the 'Horse track'. This pleasant short walk starts near Lochbuie Post Office. Walk westwards along the shore road to a bridge over the burn where the walk to Carsaig is signposted. Go through the gate on your right immediately after this and go up the hill to the farm passing above the outbuildings and out onto the hillside beyond. This is also the start of the old right of way over the hill to Rossal (see walk 10). After half a mile the path goes through a gap in a wall and across a burn with the craggy end of Beinn nan Gobhar rearing up ahead. Fork left here, following the wall downhill and into the oak woods. The path runs down through a wooded valley and along through the trees some 100 feet above the shore. This is a delightful walk, a secluded high level promenade among the trees which, after about a mile brings you out at Glenbyre farmhouse. Once you leave the trees, the way down is indistinct, but the roof of the farmhouse can be seen below and the path comes down a gully just a little short of it, immediately opposite the third telegraph post on the Lochbuie side of the house. If you do not wish to go so far, you can cut down to the shore road by a steep path that takes off just before the end of the trees above an area striped with old cultivation ridges. A small cairn is a marker for the descent. A brief stroll back along the coast road completes a very attractive short walk.

12. Carsaig Arches

an all day excursion

This is one of the most spectacular walks in south Mull. The Carsaig Arches are not merely one of the wonders of Mull - the four mile walk out to them passes below cliffs that are breathtaking in their height and scale and tenanted by deer, wild goats, ravens and eagles. They are, however, four very long and rough miles and, in certain conditions of sudden thaw, some danger may be expected from rockfalls.

The Carsaig cliffs from Carsaig pier

Starting from just above the pier at Carsaig, take the track through the trees and round the shore of the bay. The track degenerates but at the fence, do not cross the stile but go down and walk along the top of the shore to make it easier to cross the two burns. Once the western side of the bay is reached, the path is reasonable and planks have been laid over the worst of the muddy places.

Just over an hour's walking brings you to the Nun's Pass, the only place in a three-mile stretch of coastline where the great rampart of cliff is breached and a steep grassy slope gives access to the moorland above. A curious Sphinx-like rock stands on the shore below the pass and a little on the Carsaig side of this, tucked in behind a low bank, is the Nun's Cave where the nuns are reputed to have taken refuge after being driven from Iona. Crosses of various designs, some of which may go back to the 6th-9th centuries are carved on the walls. These must be picked out from amongst much ugly modern graffiti. There are also several dates, the earliest being 1633, a carving of a sailing ship, and mason's marks which date from the time when this cave was used by stonemasons working the sandstone cut from the tidal stretch just in front of the cave. This easily worked buff or greenish stone was used in parts of Iona Abbey and other church buildings. These quarries were worked from the early middle ages and thereafter intermittently throughout the centuries, the last reopening being in 1875 when stone was used in the restoration work at Iona Abbey.

Nearly two hours more brings the walker to the arches, the scenery getting increasingly grand with waves breaking over the rocks and distant views to Jura, Islay and Colonsay. Above is a jagged skyline with crumbling cliffs soaring up to nearly a thousand feet. Beyond Malcolm's Point the path comes to an abrupt and dramatic end above a rock inlet where the sea rolls in towards the first and more massive of the two arches.

Once this arch has been sufficiently admired and photographed from this point, you should retrace your steps to a small stream where a goat track leads up the gully and up over the arch - a good and level path but affording no protection whatsoever against the sheer drop to the sea. One step off the path would put the walker in a totally irretrievable position, but this is the only way to get down to the beach and stand beneath the great arch. These arches were originally sea caves which have been eroded right through the rock to form a tunnel and the great arch is 140 feet from one end to the other. The second of the two arches is taller and more slender and sports a stack at the top like a chimney.

The return can be made by the same route or, outside the stalking season (mid-August to mid-October, see note 3 on Deer, Page 4) by continuing a little further steadily climbing towards Gorrie's Leap (Binnein Ghorrie) the next break in the rampart of cliff. This also is not a route for the faint-hearted and it is best to climb as high as possible on the east of this gully before entering it to avoid too much scrambling in this very loose and unstable ground. Gorrie was a clansman of MacLaine of Lochbuie who, when savagely punished by his chief for a trivial offence, took terrible revenge by seizing Lochbuie`s baby son and, with the baby in his arms, leapt to destruction off the top of the cliff.

The walk along the top of the cliff is pleasant and easy. At the lowest point of the cliffs, where a stream goes over the cliff with a wall beyond it, Gamhnach Mhor comes into line with the east point of Rubha na Faoilinn. This is the top of the Nun's Pass. Descend the pass and return along the shore to Carsaig Pier.

13. Carsaig to Lochbuie

6 miles, 3 hours

This is one of the best known walks in south Mull, taking you along a varied and interesting shoreline. The distance by car from Carsaig to Lochbuie is twenty-five miles, along the shore route a mere six. In times gone by, most travel was by sea, but there was once an attempt to build a shore route and the evidence may be found in the occasional sections of constructed path. Start from Carsaig Pier at the notice "Public Footpath to Lochbuie." At first the path is enclosed as it passes through woodland and in places is muddy, but planks and stones help you to avoid the worst spots and the sea is soon reached. The section from here to the isolated stack called An Dunan is the most spectacular on the walk as you pick your way between the hollow cliffs and the sea. On windy days the rock face throws back the echo of the sea. Shallow caves, carved by the sea in the time of higher sea levels, run in under these cliffs, some with walls built across the entrance to be used as sheep fanks.

Beyond An Dunan the path switches between the rocky shore and the wooded skirts of the cliff. There is a sharp contrast between the wild coast with its tidal pools, and the sheltered dells where the stones are covered with thick and prolific moss. At the edge of the sea are oystercatchers and cormorants, while the woods are home to tits and wrens.

The going gets harder in the centre section of this walk, with some scrambling among the boulders, especially at high tide, to avoid the sea spray thrown up canyons and clefts in the rocks. At An Cui`Leim a rib of rock runs out preventing further progress by normal means, but there is a length of rope hanging down a ten foot drop to help walkers negotiate this place. Even at the lowest tide it is not possible to avoid this drop, but it is in no way difficult and even a small child can climb up or down with the help of the rope.

After this, the walking becomes easier and more open, with the cliffs further back from the edge of the sea. The walker is now coming in from an exposed coast to a sheltered and peaceful bay where the vegetation is more lush and the shoreline less dramatic. Just before Glenbyre there are two fields with a bridge over the Glenbyre Burn in the top corner of the first of them. From the farm a good track takes you the last mile and a half to Lochbuie.

As this walk needs to be done as a two-car exercise, or by retracing the entire route to the beginning, a circuit can be made by leaving the track a mile before the rope, where a stone wall goes uphill beside a burn. Climb steadily up until you reach the summit of Ben Carsaig (449m). The extensive views from the top of this hill across to the cliffs above the Carsaig Arches and out to sea are well worth the climb. From the summit aim for the lochan, then bear NW to reach the road. Turn left at the road and walk down the long hill to the start at Carsaig Pier, passing the red phone box made famous in the film "I Know Where I'm Going".

14. Corra Bheinn and Cruachan Dearg

Two Grahams in a day - each 704m (2300ft) 6 hours
Stalking: telephone 0131 226 2500

If Ben More and the Chioch dominate the view as you travel eastwards out of Glen More, Cruachan Dearg and Corra Bhein, twin peaks with a deep saddle between, dominate the view when entering Glen More from the west. A traverse of these two peaks makes a reasonably short, fairly strenuous day out and can be timed to co-ordinate with the ferry and the Iona buses if planning a day excursion from Oban.

Start in Glen More, where the Allt Ghillecaluim goes under the road - there is a neat space for one car to park. Go through the gap in the fence where a wicket gate once stood and walk up the west side of the burn. It is steep all the way but there are numerous grassy places, ideal for picnics, where you can draw breath and look back at the road seeing the cars looking smaller and smaller. The attractive series of waterfalls is a feature of this section of the walk, but despite the endless flow of water the rocks have not been worn away, nor have deep pools formed, because the basalt rock is so very hard. Near the top there is a long stretch of about 100 feet where the water rushes down a slope, like a flume in a swimming pool. There are two gullies to cross, but it is easy to find a way down and up the steep sides. After about an hour you will have reached a flattish grassy area.

As the gradient begins to relent on the approach to the col, take a slant leftwards up the hill to avoid the boggy ground in the col and pick your way up steep grass tongues and across scree slopes to the top of the ridge. This is probably one of the most unrelenting steep slopes on Mull, but there is ample reward as soon as you gain the ridge. Suddenly and dramatically all the major hills of Mull are on view and the trig pillar is only a short walk away. From there a wonderful panorama can be seen - not only south towards Ben Buie and the sea but also all the hills to the north and west.

Pause at the trig pillar and get your breath back before setting off in a NW direction, first down the steep side of Corra Bheinn then across and up the equally demanding ascent of Cruachan Dearg, 500 feet down, and 500 feet up again. In poor visibility, take note of the wind as a direction indicator, because there is a pronounced magnetic anomaly at the top. This should take you about an hour and a half from summit to summit - no allowance

Ben More and the Chioch from Cruachan Dearg.

made for picnics, photography or serious bird watching, but ravens, buzzards and possibly an eagle might well be added to your "ticklist" here, especially if the weather changes from showery to bright and sunny, always a good opportunity to see wildlife coming out of shelter after the rain.

Cruachan Dearg and Corra Bheinn are both classified as "Grahams" - a summit of between 2000 and 2500 feet, and now you have had the satisfaction of achieving two in one day. From the summit of Cruachan Dearg, descend to the pass, the Mam Clachaig, marked by Carn Cul Righ Albainn, a substantial cairn. From here, it is possible to turn right and walk down through Glen Clachaig to Loch Ba and along to Knock - a two-car option to vary this walk (see Walk 7). However, to return to the start, turn left and walk down the well worn path, once a busy route linking north and south Mull, to the road in Glen More. There are numerous burns to ford but there are always convenient boulders to make hopping over the water quite easy. Fairly near the end of the path there is a group of ruined buildings, the remains of Airigh Teanga Brideig, a typical shieling where the women and children of the family spent the summer, grazing the cattle and making a store of cheese and butter for the winter months. Just after that the path takes a zigzag - but carry on to the bridge at Teanga Brideig rather than be tempted to take off at a slant towards the starting point as it is a really tough slog through boggy ground.

ISHRIFF

CANNOC

LOCH AN ELLAN

LOCH AIRDEGLAS

BRIDGE

△717m

BEN BUIE

LOCH BUIE

N

CRAIG

R. COLADOIR

DERRYNACULEN

LOCH FUARAN

BEINN NAN GOBHAR △

CRUACH NAN △ CON

GLEN BYRE

A849

MAM AN △ TROTANAICH

ROSSAL

KINLOCH

LOCH SCRIDAIN

B8035

1 mile

34

15. Rossal Circuit
Rossal to Loch Buie

7 miles, 5 hours

5 miles, 3 hours

Start near the head of Loch Scridain, about halfway between the Kinloch Hotel and the junction with the B8035, at a gate marked Rossal Farm.

Walk up the farm lane and go through the gate just short of the farm, turn left on to the forestry track until, on reaching a sheep fank, take the grass grown track to the right up the hill. Some way up this, a gate gives entrance to a forestry plantation. Continue on a well trodden footpath going steadily uphill through the trees until beyond the plantation and out onto the open hill - from here the Mam Trotanaich, a shallow pass over the hills, is within easy reach. At the top of the pass, the walker is rewarded with the fine views towards Loch Buie and over the Firth of Lorn.

To complete the circuit traverse eastwards and climb Cruach nan Con, with its fine view of the Mull hills, and then drop down the western side of Torr a Ghoai to the attractive small Lochan na Cruaiche. From here it is most important to choose the correct line of descent as two forestry deer fences stretch right around the foot of the hill from Rossal to the Abhainn Loch Fuaran.

There are no stiles, gates or other means of crossing these fences but there is a gap between them directly above Derrynaculen: a corridor of hill which can be reached by setting off directly due west from Lochan na Cruaiche. An isolated boulder on the skyline is a marker for the route down, but it must be emphasised that the walker should keep well up - keep heading due west for the mouth of Loch Scridain. Do not be tempted to skirt the base of the Cruach Doire nan Cuilean, as this will lead you over the lip of the Leathad Mor - in Gaelic, the great slope, though the great wall might be a better description for this face of precipitous slab and vertical vegetation.

Over it flows a very fine waterfall fed by four burns, the last two close together running in steep gullies. Keep up and, in mist, count them carefully before beginning the descent. When you are standing at the top of the steep but grassy slope of the Leathad an Fola, you will see clearly below you the ruined walls of the old farm of Derrynaculen, birthplace of Dugald MacPhail the Gaelic bard who composed the famous song *An t'Eilean Muileach*. Descend the slope, turn left on the rough road, pass through the gate, and so back to Rossal.

Alternative route to Lochbuie from the Mam Trotanaich.

Descend eastwards, taking a line on the summit of Ben Buie, to reach the dramatic gash which marks the head of Glen Byre. Drop down to Loch Buie by following, in reverse, the route down the east side of Glen Byre described in paragraph five of the Ben Buie Circuit, keeping well up under the crags of Beinn nan Gobhar.

16. Ben More from south

966m, 3169 ft

Ascent over Chioch and Chioch ridge

The first part of this ascent follows, in reverse, the route of the old drove road, from Teanga Brideig in Glen More (see pages 16 and 17). Park near the Holly Tree Fank where a section of the old road crosses a bridge. Cross the bridge and go through a gate to start up the hill. The route climbs steadily up crossing small burns by neat little bridges and well made fords bottomed with large stones.

From the ancient cairn at the top of the pass, follow the broad ridge to the foot of the Chioch. Once the first few feet of scree are surmounted, the footing is by no means as uncomfortable as it appears from below, though walkers should be aware of the dangers of dislodging loose boulders and keep close together or follow separate lines up the slope. The summit is, as it appeared, the apex of a pyramid. The change of view now embraces the country to the north and east of Ben More - the undulating ridge of Ben Fhada with its craggy little summit, and the wide corrie between Ben Fhada and Ben More of which the Chioch ridge forms the back wall. This ridge has been compared to a miniature Aonach Eagach but that, though it pays tribute to its fine rocky character, is something of an exaggeration of its difficulties. In fact, you make your way along a sort of rampart with a protective wall of rock rising on one side with the occasional window looking north. However, the southward sweep into the Corrie Odhar is impressive enough for those with poor tolerance to exposure, and in windy or icy conditions the ridge should be treated with respect.

The ridge ends in a final pull up a steep rocky slope onto the summit of Ben More. It is not always clear which route the path takes at this point but there is a small, shallow gully on the south side of the hill which offers reasonable footing a good part of the way up. A final burst brings the walker tumbling right over the east side of the summit shelter cairn and lands him precipitant and puffing amongst the sandwich eaters who have already attained the top from the easy side.

Summit of Chioch and Chioch Ridge

36

Descent to the south

From the summit of Ben More, more than one route of descent is possible, though the route over the Chioch ridge is probably best only as an ascent. The most popular route to the summit starts at sea level at Dhiseig but this descent is only possible with two cars. For the walker who started at Teanga Brideig and came up over the Chioch, a descent to the south is the best variation and more or less completes a circuit.

From the summit cairn, set off due south along an open plateau with the ground failing away dramatically to the left. After the cairn, the direction turns to the south-west and the descent becomes steeper. The walker reaches Maol nan Damh after picking a way across a stretch of ground scattered with little lochans. Turning south again the descent is a steady but steep route over rough ground broken by large slabs of rock to reach the B8035 near Loch Beg. From here turn left and follow the road to just short of the Kinloch junction, turning left again to follow the old road most of the way back to Teanga Brideig.

17. Scoor

9 miles
An all-day excursion

An exploration of the south coast of the Ross of Mull, returning over moorland tops which, for all their modest height, give wonderful views back to the hills and out to the isles.

Turn off the Craignure-Fionnphort road just short of Bunessan, where Assapol House and Scoor are signposted. Park at the visitors` car park just above Kilvickeon cemetery and continue on foot on the track that leads to Scoor House. Bear left to pass in front of the big house and go through the gate. The track carries on for a while, climbing uphill to enter a field with a rectangular fank (a stone enclosure for sheep) in it. Ignore the gate below the fank and follow the track, sometimes rather faint over the grass, to the top gate. From there continue to the edge of the ridge then turn left along the ridge following a narrow track, aiming in the direction of the forest ride clearly visible across the valley. In a short while, the track to Shiaba will be spotted below you, and in a few yards along this you will see the gable end of a roofless shell said to have been the schoolhouse. Over 350 people lived here at the end of the eighteenth century and the remains of their houses and the boundary walls that marked their crofts can be seen all the way across to the wall where the forestry plantation begins.

Go through a gap in the wall to pass through a firebreak (ride) in the trees then ascend to the cliff tops. Alternatively, descend to the shore and the beaches where the emigrant ships took the people of Shiaba away in the time of the clearances. An isolated ruin here is the shop which served Shiaba, sited close to the shore for the landing of goods in bulk. Follow along the line of the forestry fence to regain the high ground - a place to have your binoculars ready for deer, eagles and wild goats - everything, in fact, that gives south Mull its unique atmosphere. It is a most exciting place to be, but there is a fairly narrow strip of ground between the fence and the cliff top and attention should be paid to where you are putting your feet as well as eagle spotting.

Eventually the deer fence turns inland and you can either follow it to a point where it has been taken down and where a faint track connects with the forest road down the middle of the plantation, or continue onto the high ground and look across to the cliffs running out to Malcolm's Point and soaring almost 1000 feet above the Carsaig Arches just visible at their foot. Halfway along where the highest point of the visible horizon juts out like a platform is Gorrie's Leap. (The tale of Gorrie's leap is on page 30). If you want to make your way to the arches from here, make the descent to the shore by the gully west of Eas Criarachain waterfall as described in Walk 18.

Now it is time to turn inland, returning to the deer fence and following it till you reach a gap which will take you out onto the higher moorland where, with height gained, all the hills of Mull come into view to the northwest. The trig pillar is not quite the highest point but the ridge from there, taking in a few false summits, to the last top is easy striding on turf and well cropped heather. Once arrived, you can start counting islands - Islay, Jura, Scarba, Lunga and the Islands of the Sea (Garvellochs), Luing and Mull, Colonsay, Staffa, Coll, Iona and Tiree. All present and correct and on a clear day you can also tick off Barra Head and, by straining your eyes and imagination, the Cuillins.

From this summit walk down towards a small cairn, then on down till a fence is reached. Go left and follow the fence until a gate into a wide firebreak is reached. Follow this firebreak downhill, crossing a forestry track on the way, until another gate opens on to a shallow valley. This valley is where the MacPhees from Colonsay once attempted a raid on Shiaba. They were to sail from Colonsay under cover of darkness but, too eager for the fat cattle of Shiaba, set off with last rays of the setting sun catching their boats. The Mull men were waiting in ambush in this valley and fell on the MacPhees, routing them and chasing them back to their boats at Port Bheathain. They were sent home to Colonsay but not before each had had his thumbs cut off to make sure that it would be no easy task to row back again. A gloomy tale if you are late off the hill, but the Shiaba track is just across the other side of the shallow valley and the last mile back to Scoor house is familiar from the route out.

The walk to Port Bheathain is a delightful short excursion in itself and is well described by the Ross of Mull Historical Society in one of their leaflets.

18. Across the Ross

An all-day walk

Stalking Season: See Code for Mull on page 4

With two cars, it is possible to link this walk with the Carsaig Arches or Scoor for a truly spectacular day out.

This walk passes easily through open country and woods and ends with an awesomely wild second section. Those who decide to do the complete circuit must be prepared for some scrambling. As with the walk to the Carsaig Arches, there is danger from rock falls in conditions of heavy rain or sudden thaw.

Start at the bend in the A849 where it crosses the Beach river: there is ample parking between the road and the sea. Cross the river by the old bridge and follow the unsurfaced road that passes below the bungalow and out onto the moor through a gate. The walking is less monotonous than one might be led to expect from the map and there is a fine waterfall in the eponymous Allt an Easa Mhoir. The track goes through a shallow ford at the top of the waterfall. A hundred yards on, pass through a side gate into the forestry plantation. Within the plantation the walking is reasonably open as the trees do not crowd the road and the planting is mixed with spruce, larch and pine. There is a tempting view ahead to the spectacular rock bastion of Ben Gorrie a rugged hilltop surmounted by a turret of rock. The view of this cliff top gets more dramatic as the walker goes on.

At the end of the trees, a stile takes the walker over the deer fence and onto an older but still firm track, and soon the sea comes into view. As the path splits, bear to the right towards a group of ruins. These are named on the map Airigh Mhic Cribhain, but all appear to have been more substantial buildings than one would expect of an airigh or shieling. A shieling was a dwelling used only in the summer when the cattle were taken to more remote pastures to graze, far away from the growing crops. Here, too, the women would make butter and cheese. The buildings were usually small huts roofed with heather and the remains found are often scanty. In this group there is also evidence of a stackyard and a corn-drying kiln. Those with an interest in deserted villages may well feel happy to have reached journey's end. Those whose taste runs more to geological time rather than historical should prepare to descend to the shore down through the layers of the tertiary volcanic ages.

From this group of buildings walk to an old fence which runs down towards the burn. Then continue, with the fence on the right and the burn on the left. Where the fence crosses the burn, cross the fence (but not the burn) and carry on to the top of the cliffs. Suddenly you will come to the top of a waterfall, the Eas Criarachan, but it may announce itself earlier by clouds of spray if a strong wind is blowing up the cliff.

After admiring the views of the cliffs and the sea and the distant islands from this airy vantage point, the walker can either retreat and retrace his route to the start, or extend the walk by descending to sea level. Work westwards along the cliff to find a steep gully leading clean down to the shore (though there is quite a lot of loose scree in the middle so walk down the side of the gully, keeping together if walking in a group).

From the bottom it is possible to pick a way back along the shore to the waterfall and round into the deep bay called the Traigh Cadh an Easa, which offers a stretch which is easier on the ankles. The cliffs soar above the walker and on windy days the sound of the sea echoing off the steep face can be quite deafening.

Beyond, the going is slightly easier if the walker navigates along the aerial trackways of the deer and wild goats who are the proper residents of this domain (it is claimed that the goats have been there since the days of the Spanish Armada). These game trails run across the slope almost like visible contour lines, but by working gently upwards from one to another the walker will slowly gain height. All the time, though, the cliff top is also gaining height until at Gorrie's Leap its crenellated lip is over 900 feet above the sea. You begin to feel you have entered a lost world and if you do not see a pterodactyl come over the cliffs you will very probably see an eagle.

Gorrie's Leap

41

Wild goats at Carsaig

Gorrie's Leap (for story see page 30) is the last possible way back to the world above for the next three miles and the game trails lead faithfully up it - the centre hump between the two washouts is probably the easiest route. Once at the top, the Airigh Mhic Chriabhan is not difficult to pick out. As you approach this old settlement you may be interested to know that there is a seam of inferior coal nearby which has been casually worked in recent times. From here it is down the slope and back to the track to amble home, enjoying the open views across Loch Scridain to Ben More and the other hills of central Mull.

Eas Criarachan

19. Erraid

A visit to a tidal island with literary associations.

For those who have read *Kidnapped*, Erraid will always be the island where the shipwrecked David Balfour to his chagrin spent four wet and miserable days living off shellfish because he did not realise that the island was tidal. But Stevenson used the island in other stories as well and, on a sparkling day in spring or summer one might believe his early acquaintance with the emerald seas, the pattern of reefs and the warm red rocks of the Ross of Mull fired his imagination for the South Seas and the story of *Treasure Island*, the chart of which, "struck out by J Hawkins" bears more than a little resemblance to Erraid.

At low tide you can walk down from Knockvologan Farm and cross the sandbank between the low granite cliffs dryshod. The channel is about a quarter of a mile in length and should be continued to its northern end and round the coast to the buildings that formed the shore base for the construction of Dhu Heartach lighthouse. The houses and outbuildings were built for the lighthouse keepers and their families and the present day occupants use the gardens and storage to be similarly self-sufficient. Skirting round these it is an easy climb past the signal station, once used to communicate with the lighthouse, to the highest point (no trig pillar now) and stand imagining how it must have felt to be marooned on this island with neither food nor shelter as described in RLS's story.

He was one of the great Stevenson family of lighthouse engineers and as a student he spent time here during the building of the lighthouse. This light, which may be seen 15 miles out to the SW is 126 feet high and marks a treacherous rock less than 50 feet above sea level in the middle of the passage up the Firth of Lorn. Closer to you are the notorious Torran rocks where David Balfour was wrecked and between the outermost of the islands to the SW you may see yachts lying in Tinker's Hole, the last secure anchorage for boats heading round the south coast of Mull. Across the water lie the marble quarries of Iona and, to the NW the Abbey, always a conspicuous landmark in the southern part of Mull.

From the top of the hill return by striding across the heathery uplands and around the granite torrs to reach the sandbank crossing before the tide comes in (tide tables can be obtained from chandlers and shops).

David Balfour continued his adventures by walking across Mull, presumably through Glen More, though Stevenson takes some writer's liberties with distances and has him meet a selection of colourful characters on the way before he finally reaches the inn at Craignure (then called Torosay).

20. Fionnphort Quarries   *2 miles, 1 hour*

The Fionnphort or Tormore quarries are only a short walk from the Iona ferry landing place. This is one of six quarries that were operating in the Ross last century.

A quarter of a mile along the main road from Fionnphort village is a track leading north past Bruach Mhor. The track goes up the hill behind the buildings and almost immediately you come upon the old quarry workings. The quarry was closed about 1910 and until 1987 there were huge blocks of cut granite, some seven feet by four feet, stacked ready for shipment at the point when commercial working stopped. Recently the quarry has been re-opened, the blocks removed and some limited working takes place. Further exploration brings you to the main quarry area, where a long tramway led down to the pier. The stone was once exported to many parts of Britain, and even the USA, before competition and transport costs grew too high. It may be seen in London, Liverpool and Glasgow: the Holburn Viaduct, the Liverpool Docks and Jamaica Bridge were constructed using this rich pink granite, which was also used extensively in buildings throughout Mull for facings and lintels. Most recently it was considered for use in the extension to the House of Commons, but the most accessible stone proved, when tested, to be flawed and the expense of extracting high quality granite from the floor of the quarry was considered too great. In the main hall of the Aberdeen Art Galleries there are pillars of different coloured granites from all over Scotland, including one from the Ross of Mull.

Just off the pier is a safe anchorage known as the Bull Hole. sheltered by Eilean nam Ban (Island of the Women), to which Columba is said to have banished women from Iona, suspecting they might cause trouble!

Return to the start of the walk by the same route.

Dressed blocks of granite on the old pier.

21. Camas Tuath   *3 miles, 2 hours*

Another short outing in the Ross of Mull.

Leave the road half a mile west of Ardfenaig where a gate just past a footbridge opens onto a track. After a second gate, follow the track north across the open moorland where peat cutting still takes place. After half a mile the track bends to the right through rocky outcrops and soon a fine wall, built 'Galloway` style, borders the track all the way down to the bay called Camus Tuath. An adventure camp for young people makes use of the old buildings, still without electricity, near the shore, originally built to house workers at the quarries across the bay. The buildings can easily be seen from the quarry across the bay, so just as the roofs of these buildings come into sight turn right through a gap in the wall and head across the marshy ground until you come to the saltings, a low lying grassy area covered at very high tides. At the head of an inlet of the sea. The remains of a wall marks the head of this inlet and across it a path goes uphill roughly at right angles to the wall. Follow this path as it winds steadily uphill until you reach the quarry. A green and white post marks the entrance to the quarry workings.

In the quarry, drill holes and other evidence of working can be clearly seen. The remains of the tramway lead down the hillside from the quarry to the pier from which the granite was shipped. This is still in reasonably good order being built of this hard stone. The granite here is a pale flesh colour, not as pink as that from the quarries at Fionnphort and has a coarse-grained texture. Blocks were used to build Skerryvore (1844) and Ardnamurchan (1845) lighthouses which were designed by Alan Stevenson, uncle of the writer Robert Louis. The Skerryvore reef, pounded by the full force of the

Atlantic, lies 10 miles southwest of Tiree, right in the path of vessels making for the Clyde and Mersey. Stevenson's estimate for the time it took to dress each stone for the outside of the tower was 120 man hours. Internal stones took longer - 320 hours. The granite blocks were so accurately prepared that when they were shipped to the reef they fitted together perfectly. The total operation lasted a year and a half and used 5000 tons of granite. If you want to go across the top of the quarry, to get a good view across to the buildings and out to sea to Staffa and the north, a line of green and white posts gives warning of the steep drop. Return to the start by retracing your route back to the wall and the track.

22. Ardtun
2 miles, 1½ hours

This is a short geological excursion from Bunessan with easy walking. The leaf beds of Ardtun were first described by the then Duke of Argyll in a paper in the Quarterly Journal of the Geological Society of London on January 8, 1851. They are composed of the leaves of (mainly) deciduous trees, falling autumn after autumn into the waters of a prehistoric lake and there becoming fossilised by a process so gentle that even today the leaf beds resemble nothing so much as narrow bands of leaf mould set between gravels and sand.

From Bunessan take the road signposted to Ardtun and follow this till you come to a fork. Bear left along the road by the shore and park on the right-hand side, just before the last two houses are reached where the road goes over a culvert. From here, the most attractive course is to walk to the little flat-topped outcrop of Dunan Mor with its conspicuous cairn. Carry straight on, descending to the shore. The most interesting way follows the coast, though there is an easier and less dramatic route along the top of the little cliffs.

On the lower route there are interesting coastal features, notably stands of columnar basalt. In the distance you may see Staffa where columnar basalt is to be seen at its most impressive and regular. Sheep tracks take you along under the low basalt cliffs, passing round the precipitous head of a chasm with the sea surging into it and bringing you to a deep, narrow inlet likewise precipitous at the head. Here you are forced up to regain the top of the cliffs. Now cut across the headland looking north-eastwards towards the soaring mass of Ardmeanach. In a very short while you will reach the top of another gully easy of access at its head. This gully is completely dry, well above the sea and strewn with fallen rocks.

In the sides of this valley are the fossilised leaf beds which were first seen for what they were by the Duke of Argyll. The leaf beds are visible as recessed bands where years of scraping by fossil hunters have worn the layers away. Samples represent a temperate flora with leaves of hazel, plane and oak trees and are indicative of the climate here in the Eocene era (about 54 million years ago).

Return by the same route - the moor is wet, boggy and generally less attractive than the shore.

FOSSIL

LEAF VEINS

23. Iona

Two short walks

The sacred Isle of Iona is known throughout the world and thousands of people visit it every year, making a pilgrimage to its ancient abbey and precincts. This is all well described in other guides and not within the scope of this book.

The island is a small piece of the Outer Isles dropped off at the end of the long arm which is the Ross of Mull. The distinctive pink granites of the Ross cease at Fionnphort and Lewisian gneiss, the rock of the Western Isles. takes over to form, in Iona, an island of humps and hollows: "little rocky hills, with narrow verdant hollows between...numerous enough for every recluse to take his solitary walk, undisturbed by society," says Thomas Pennant, who visited Iona in 1774 - a walker's quotation to stand beside that of a more famous visitor: "That man is little to be envied, whose patriotism would not gain force upon the plain of Marathon, or whose piety would not grow warmer among the ruins of Iona" (Samuel Johnson).

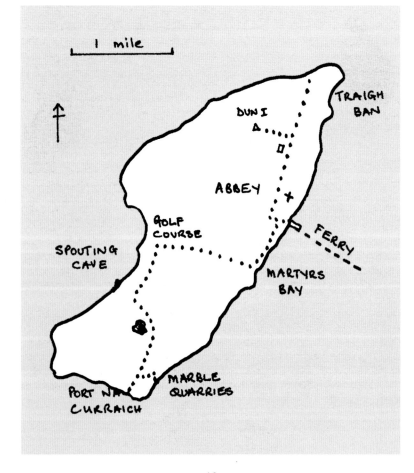

Walk 1

Leaving the ferry, turn left and follow the tarmac road past Martyrs Bay and Traigh Mor. Continue on the road as it turns up the hill and comes eventually to a gate. Through the gate you come on a stretch of machair - short, springy turf growing on a base of windblown shell sand. Machair is a special habitat found on the Atlantic coasts of the islands of Scotland and, being rich in lime, affords sheep and cattle good grazing. Here you will see a few of the holes of the Iona golf course originally laid out as nine holes in 1895, and extended to eighteen in 1905.

Walk over the springy turf towards the pebbly shore to look across to the Spouting Cave, a natural curiosity from which, with a good westerly swell running, a burst of white water and a plume of spray rises high up the cliff. When the cave is in good form this plume can be clearly seen from the summit of Dun I, two miles away.

From the shore, follow the track that leads due south over the hill, keeping the lochan on your right and then on down to Port na Cuiraich, known as St Columba's Bay. It was here that St Columba landed in his boat in 563 AD. A long mound of earth is said to mark the size of his boat and shingle from the shore has been heaped to form a multitude of cairns - no one knows the age or origin of these, though another tradition has it that these were the penitential cairns of monks, set to raise heaps equal to their sins.

Before leaving the bay, a hunt along the beach could produce little green pebbles but, if disappointed here, a visit to the marble quarries might yield a small piece of Iona marble with, perhaps, a small vein of the green serpentine for which the marble was once so famous.

To find the quarries, retrace your steps to the back of the level greensward and turn right (due east) up a heathery gully with low but steep cliffs on each side. Keep on in this direction till you come to a hollow with, tucked away to the right, the footing of two small buildings. One was an old cottage and the other the foundation for a hut used as living quarters by the quarrymen. Bearing right you will find the skeletal remains of a producer-gas engine manufactured by Fielding & Platt of Gloucester, and a cutting-frame by G.Anderson of Arbroath. These pieces of machinery have recently been coated to preserve them from rusting away. The structures remaining are a small dam cut into the rock and a gunpowder store. At the water's edge a steep-sided rock acted as a landing-stage in calm weather for boats taking away the stone. Rusty stanchions are still firmly embedded in the rock. The quarries were worked at various times from early days, the last period of activity lasting from 1907 until shortly after the outbreak of the first world war. To complete the walk, retrace your steps to Columba's Bay and return by the path and across the golf course and down the road to the ferry. Iona marble has been used in many places but to see it truly impressive slab visit the Abbey where the communion table is entirely constructed of marble from these quarries.

Port na Curaich

Walk 2

Another walk is to the top of Iona's highest hill, Dun-I. Continue past the Abbey until you reach a large white house with seven dormer windows called Bishops Walk. Just past this is a small gate into a field - cross the field

and clamber up the rocky slope to the summit. From the top of Dun-I the island is spread out around you and the hills of Mull and other more distant islands, such as Jura and its three Paps, can be seen. Also on the horizon to the SW is Dhu Heartach lighthouse and thirty miles away to the west, just visible on a good day, the remote Skerryvore lighthouse.

Returning to the road by the same path, you can explore a little farther by turning left and walking along till you reach the beautiful white sands of Traigh Bhan, another of Iona's lovely beaches.

Marble Quarries

24. Kinloch Ford

It seems fitting to end this book with a short walk that finishes at a pub. The Kinloch Ford was used to cut off the two miles round the head of Loch Scridain. Rapid and exceptionally thirsty walkers can even beat the car round to the pub if dropped at the north side of the loch directly opposite the Kinloch Hotel. Walk alongside the spit of land until you come to a post - the route lies between this post and the post on the south side in front of the hotel. In the days before the motor car, this was a well-used route for carts, animals and people on foot. When the Coladoir is in spate, the middle of the ford will be knee-depth and it goes without saying that this should only be attempted at low tide!

Further Reading

Other publications from Brown and Whittaker:
Walking in North Mull Companion volume to this.
Mull: Monuments and History, An excursion guide to standing stones and archaeological sites.
The Wildlife of Mull, and how to find it, Jay Butler & Anna Levin
Mull Family Names for Ancestor Hunters, Jo Currie.
MacLeans, a Biographical Dictionary, Jo Currie.
Traditional Tales of Mull, Peter Macnab.
A Treasure Lost, the Spanish Armada Wreck in Tobermory Bay, Olive Brown and Jean Whittaker.
Through the Year with St Columba, a Celtic prayer for every week.

Ross of Mull
The Ross of Mull Historical Society have put together a series of leaflets describing short walks of local and historical interest in the Ross of Mull and these will take you into interesting corners of that part of Mull.

Novels and Films
Annabel Carothers, *Kilcaraig*. Family saga of three generations of Mull landowners. A good read.
Elisabeth Luard, *Emerald*.

Robert Louis Stevenson. *Kidnapped*. (Walk no 19)
Archie Roy, *Sable Night*. Supernatural thriller set on Mull.
I Know Where I'm Going, Cult movie (1945) starring Wendy Hiller (Walks no 11 & 13).
Jessica Stirling *The Island Wife, The Wind from the Hills, The Strawberry Season*.
Renate Dorrestein, *A Crying Shame*.

Natural History Reference Books.
J.E. Richey, *The Tertiary Volcanic Districts*.
Rosalind Jones, *Mull in the Making. The geology of Mull*.
Richard Fitter, Alastair Fitter and Marjorie Blamey, *The Wild Flowers of Britain and
    Northern Europe*.
A.C. Jermy and J.C. Crabbe, *The Island of Mull. Flora* (British Museum 1978). Detailed
    and specialised.
Lars Svensson, *Birds of Europe*.
P Hayman, *Birdwatchers Pocket Guide*. Well-produced and, in slim format, truly a pocket guide.
Mike Madders and Philip Snow, *Birds of Mull*.
Hamlyn Guide, *Seashores and Shallow Seas of Britain and Europe*.
Whittet Guides: *Otters, Deer, Eagles, Puffins, Seals, Whales*

General
Mull HMSO: *Argyll 3* (Mull, Tiree etc), and Argyll 4 (Iona): RCAHMS Detailed and specialised.
Jo Currie, *Mull: the Island and its People*.
Meg Douglass, *Lost Townships, Silent Voices* Gazetteer of Mull settlements.
N. Hesketh. *The Story of Mull and Iona*. A historical interpretation through the eyes of an artist.
Hilary Peel, *Isle of Mull. Iona and Staffa*.
P.A. Macnab, *Mull & Iona*.
P.A. Macnab, *Highways and Byways in Mull*.
Christine Wiener, Mull, *A Traveller's Guide*.
Nicholas MacLean-Bristol, *Warriors and Priests, the History of the Clan Maclean. 1300-1570*.
Nicholas Maclean-Bristol, *Murder Under Trust*.
Charles Maclean, *The Isle of Mull, Placenames, Meanings and Stories*.

Relevant to specific walks (walk nos. in brackets)
Samuel Johnson & James Boswell. *Journey to the Western Islands of Scotland and Journal of a
    Tour to the Hebrides (23)*.
Joan Faithfull, *The Ross of Mull Granite Quarries* (20, 21)
David Viner, *The Iona Marble Quarry* (23)
Robert Louis Stevenson, *The New Lighthouse on the Dhu Heartach Rock. Argyllshire* (19).
Bella Bathurst, *The Lighthouse Stevensons*. (19)
Eunice Wilson, *Night on Ben Talaidh*, wartime aircrash and dramatic rescue, (5).
Jackie LeMay & Joanna Gardner, *Glen More, a drive through history* (1)
Margaret Macdonald, *Lachann Dubh a'Chrogain*, Poems with supporting anecdotes, bilingual (2)

Other walking guides
SMC: The Munros
The Corbetts
The Islands of Scotland including Skye

First published 1987
Printed by Nevisprint, Fort William